THE STORY OF THE
SACRAMENTO
KINGS

CREATIVE ● EDUCATION

Published by Creative Education
123 South Broad Street
Mankato, Minnesota 56001
Creative Education is an imprint of The Creative Company.

DESIGN AND PRODUCTION BY **EVANSDAY DESIGN**

PHOTOGRAPHS BY Getty Images (Bill Baptist / NBAE, Andrew D.
Bernstein / NBAE, Stephen Dunn, Garrett Ellwood / NBAE, Focus
on Sport, Walter Iooss Jr. / NBAE, Jed Jacobsohn, Yale Joel /
Time Life Pictures, Lewis Kemper, Fernando Medina / NBAE,
NBA Photo Library, NBAE Photos, Don Smith / NBAE, Peter
Stackpole / Time Life Pictures, Rocky Widner / NBAE)

LIBRARY OF CONGRESS CATALOGING-IN-PUBLICATION DATA

LeBoutillier, Nate.
The story of the Sacramento Kings / by Nate LeBoutillier.
p. cm. — (The NBA—a history of hoops)
Includes index.
ISBN-13: 978-1-58341-423-1
1. Sacramento Kings (Basketball team)—History—
Juvenile literature. I. Title. II. Series.

GV885.52.S24L43 2006
796.323'64'0979454—dc22   2005051769

First edition

9 8 7 6 5 4 3 2 1

COVER PHOTO: *Mike Bibby*

THE STORY OF THE
SACRAMENTO
KINGS

NATE LeBOUTILLIER

CREATIVE ● EDUCATION

The crowd thunders.

SOLD-OUT ARCO ARENA TEEMS ONCE AGAIN WITH
SACRAMENTO KINGS FOLLOWERS WHO SHOUT, STOMP,
CLAP, AND EVEN BANG ON COWBELLS. THE SCORE IS
KNOTTED WHEN THE KINGS COMMIT A FOUL IN THE
GAME'S FINAL SECONDS. AS AN OPPOSING PLAYER STEPS
TO THE FREE-THROW LINE, THE ARCO CROWD SWELLS
LIKE A CRASHING OCEAN, TRYING TO RATTLE HIM. THE
PLAYER AT THE LINE WIPES HIS BROW. WILL HE MAKE
IT? WILL HE MISS? IF HE MISSES BECAUSE OF THE NOISE,
THE PRESSURE, IT WON'T BE THE FIRST TIME A KINGS
CROWD AFFECTED A GAME'S OUTCOME.

A ROYAL BIRTH

IN 1839, A SWISS PIONEER NAMED JOHN SUTTER built a small fort along the Sacramento River in central California. In the 1860s, the fort grew into a town called Sacramento, which gained fame as a key terminal for America's first cross-country railroad and the famous Pony Express. Over the years, Sacramento became a destination point for many, and in 1985, a professional basketball team also moved to Sacramento. That team— the Kings of the National Basketball Association (NBA)— had a long history of travel.

One of the elite scorers of the 1950s, Jack Twyman was renowned for his accurate shooting touch.

The Kings franchise began in New York in 1945 as the Rochester Royals. Led by guards Bob Davies and Red Holzman, the Royals captured the National Basketball League (NBL) championship in their first year. They stayed near the top of the NBL for two more seasons, then moved to the Basketball Association of America (BAA) in 1948. The next season, the NBA was formed, and the Royals joined their third league.

The Royals might have gone down in history as the best team in the early years of the NBA had it not been for George Mikan, the Minneapolis Lakers' 6-foot-10 center. "When I started playing with Rochester, it was either us or Minneapolis that would win it all," said Davies. "They had the big men and we had the good little men. That was the difference in a nutshell. It was murder playing against Mikan because when the Lakers needed two points, he'd get them. George Mikan cost me a lot of money in playoff bonuses and endorsements."

In the 1951 playoffs, though, Mikan was out of action with a broken foot, and the Royals finally topped the Lakers to reach the NBA Finals. Led by Davies, guard Bobby Wanzer, and center Arnie Risen, the Royals then beat the New York Knicks in a close series to claim their first NBA championship.

The Royals continued to play well, but they needed new talent. They found some in 1955, drafting center Maurice Stokes and forward Jack Twyman. Stokes was an immediate star, leading Rochester in virtually every statistical category in his first season. Over the next three years, he and Twyman also emerged as top-flight scorers. Still, the team struggled. With fan attendance low, the Royals' owners decided to move the team to Cincinnati, Ohio, in 1957.

The Royals had better luck in Cincinnati, making the playoffs in 1958, but those would be Stokes and Twyman's last games together. Late in the 1957–58 season, Stokes fell and hit his head on the floor during a game. Days later, doctors discovered that he had suffered brain damage, a condition that soon left him paralyzed.

THE TWYMAN AND STOKES STORY

"You'll never know, meet, or read about anybody as courageous as Maurice," said Jack Twyman. "I never heard the man complain in 12 years of lying on his back." Maurice Stokes, the NBA's Rookie of the Year in 1955–56 with the Rochester Royals, played three stellar seasons, averaging 16.4 points and 17.3 rebounds per game. But in 1958, Stokes banged his head on the floor during a game, later fell into a coma, and was paralyzed. Twyman and Stokes had grown up together in Pittsburgh, Pennsylvania, and they were both drafted by the Royals in 1955, so it was no surprise that Twyman came to his teammate's aid. Twyman even became Stokes's legal guardian, taking great care of him until he died in 1970. Today, both players are enshrined in the Basketball Hall of Fame.

13

Dynamic center Maurice Stokes played only three pro seasons, earning All-Star status every year.

FROM "THE BIG O" TO "TINY"

TWO YEARS AFTER STOKES'S TRAGIC INJURY, TWYMAN was paired with another explosive talent: sensational guard Oscar Robertson. Known as "The Big O," Robertson joined the Royals in 1960 and set the league on fire. "Don't try to describe the man," Twyman once said of Robertson. "You can watch him, you can enjoy him, you can appreciate him, but you can't adequately describe him. It's not any one thing—it's his completeness that amazes you."

Robertson's brilliance seemed to elevate his teammates as well. Twyman became a perennial All-Star, and center Wayne Embry added strength in the paint. In 1963, Cincinnati also drafted outstanding center Jerry Lucas. But in both 1963 and 1964, the Boston Celtics beat the Royals in the Eastern Division Finals and went on to claim the NBA championship.

15

Whether shooting from long range or driving to the basket, Oscar Robertson was an almost unstoppable force

16

Jerry Lucas was a famously determined rebounder, averaging 15 boards a game over his Hall of Fame career.

The Royals remained a contender throughout the 1960s. Then, in 1969, Cincinnati hired former Celtics star Bob Cousy as head coach. Unfortunately, Robertson and Lucas did not take well to Cousy's coaching style, and both stars were soon traded away.

In the 1970 NBA Draft, the Royals found two new leaders: center Sam Lacey and guard Nate "Tiny" Archibald. Lacey soon established himself as one of the NBA's best rebounding centers, but it was Archibald who really surprised fans. Despite standing only 5-foot-11, the ultra-quick guard emerged as the Royals' top scoring threat.

Archibald was the engine that powered the Royals in 1972–73, becoming the first and only player to lead the NBA in points (34 per game) and assists (11.4 per game) in the same season. That year, the Royals changed their name to the Kings and began playing their home games in Kansas City, Missouri, and Omaha, Nebraska. The club finished with a 36–46 record, missing the playoffs.

BIG O'S BIG SEASON

A triple-double (recording double figures in three different statistical categories) is a sign of a great all-around individual game. When Oscar Robertson averaged a triple-double over an entire *season*, well, there were no superlatives that could describe the feat, because no one had ever even come close to doing it before. Former teammate Jerry Lucas later said, "He obviously was unbelievable, way ahead of his time. There is no more complete player than Oscar." Statistically, Lucas is right. No one has ever matched Robertson's 1961–62 averages of 30.8 points, 12.5 rebounds, and 11.4 assists per game. Renowned for his supreme athleticism, Robertson played in 12 straight NBA All-Star Games, won a title with the Milwaukee Bucks in 1970–71, and was elected to the Basketball Hall of Fame in 1979.

THE KANSAS CITY YEARS

IN 1974–75, THE KINGS FINALLY MADE THE PLAYOFFS. But when the club—which settled solely in Kansas City in 1975—faltered again the next season, the Kings traded Archibald to the New Jersey Nets for two first-round draft picks.

19

Speedy guard Phil Ford led the Kansas City Kings in assists in each of his four seasons with the team.

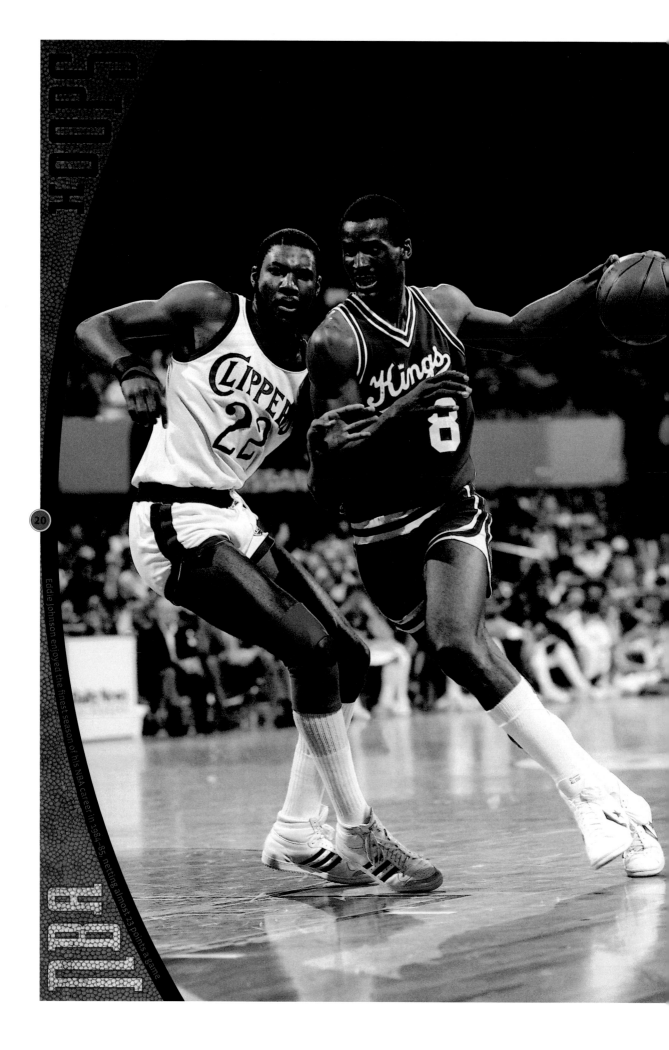

Eddie Johnson enjoyed the finest season of his NBA career in 1984–85, netting almost 22 points a game

The Kings used the picks to acquire guards Otis Birdsong and Phil Ford, who brought a new spirit to the team. "They're like two peas in a pod," said Cotton Fitzsimmons, who took over as Kings coach in 1978. "They're a couple of professional comedians who just happen to play ball in the NBA. They're the guys who keep this team loose, and you have to be loose to play basketball."

In 1978–79, Birdsong, Ford, and dependable forward Scott Wedman led Kansas City to the Midwest Division title. Two seasons later, the Kings staged a near-miracle. Although they went a mere 40–42 that year, they sneaked into the playoffs. "In terms of individual talent, I think you would have to say there is not a lot here," Fitzsimmons said. "But our club has chemistry. Nobody's going to beat us badly in the playoffs."

Unfortunately for the Kings, Ford and Birdsong went down with injuries in the playoffs, yet the team slipped past Portland and Phoenix before the Houston Rockets ended the "Cinderella" season. Surprisingly, Kings management traded Birdsong, Wedman, and Lacey mere months later for guards Eddie Johnson and Reggie Theus. The trade backfired, and Kansas City's winning chemistry evaporated.

TALENTED TINY

Whether Kings guard Nate "Tiny" Archibald shot or passed, the result was most often going to be the same—two points for his team. In 1972–73, Archibald became the only player in the history of the NBA to lead the league in both scoring (34 points per game) and assists (11.4 per game). Archibald, a wiry, left-handed speedster who later helped the Boston Celtics win the 1981 NBA championship, got his basketball start in the innards of New York City, where he grew up as the eldest of seven kids. "People say, 'Well, most people in the inner city, they're doing drugs, or they're hanging out,' and stuff like that," said Archibald. "Well, I hung out on the basketball court. I hung out in the community centers. That was my outlet."

ON TO SACRAMENTO

WHILE THE KINGS STRUGGLED IN THE EARLY 1980S, a group of businessmen in Sacramento purchased the club. In 1985, they moved it to California's growing capital. The people of Sacramento packed the stands for every home game (the Kings would sell out their arena each game of their first 13 seasons in Sacramento), and Reggie Theus and Eddie Johnson each scored more than 18 points per game to lead the 1985–86 Kings to the playoffs.

SACRAMENTO

23

Reggie Theus suited up for five different NBA teams but spent his greatest years in a Kings uniform

Like Reggie Theus, Mitch Richmond was a top-notch scorer who never saw a winning season in Sacramento to

The Kings ran out of steam the next season, falling to 29–53. The poor record triggered a series of what seemed like endless changes for Sacramento. Coaches and players—including guard Kenny Smith and forwards Antoine Carr and Wayman Tisdale—came and went over the next five years as the team struggled.

In 1992, Sacramento traded a high draft pick for Golden State Warriors guard Mitch Richmond, who became the first Kings player since Nate Archibald to start in an All-Star Game. "He's as tough as they come, both offensively and defensively," said Portland Trail Blazers guard Clyde Drexler. "He's absolutely one of the top three [shooting] guards in the NBA, and everyone in the league knows it."

The Kings tried to surround Richmond with talented players such as forward Walt Williams, but the losing continued. In 1996–97, the Kings finished with a 27–55 record. It was the team's 15th straight losing season—a dubious new NBA record.

THE KINGS' NEW THRONE

Although Sacramento is one of the NBA's smallest cities, it seems to lead the league in fan support. On October 25, 1985, the Kings—freshly moved from Kansas City to Sacramento—were scheduled to play their first game in their new home. "It reminded me of what you see before a college football game," said Kings guard Larry Drew. "It was like the boosters in the parking lot, barbecuing, throwing footballs around.... People were dressed in tuxedos, and some women were in evening gowns. They were really getting geared up for their basketball." Although the Kings lost, 108–104 to the Los Angeles Clippers, the night was deemed a success and set a precedent. Said Kings forward Eddie Johnson: "What blew me away was the fans still gave us a standing ovation even though we lost."

NEW KINGS ATTITUDE

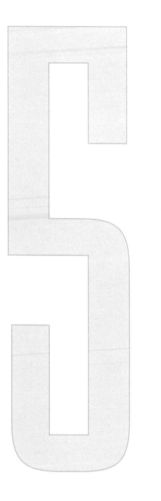

IN JANUARY 1998, THE KINGS WERE PURCHASED BY the Maloof family, who dedicated themselves to building a winner. The Maloofs quickly made a bold move, trading Richmond to the Washington Wizards for powerful young forward Chris Webber. Sacramento soon featured a new lineup (including center Vlade Divac and rookie point guard Jason Williams), a new coach (Rick Adelman), and most importantly, a new attitude.

In 1998–99, Webber averaged 20 points and a league-high 13 rebounds per game, and Coach Adelman implemented a fast-break offense that Williams ran with flashy efficiency. The end result was a 27–23 record, a playoff appearance, and a surge in the Kings' popularity.

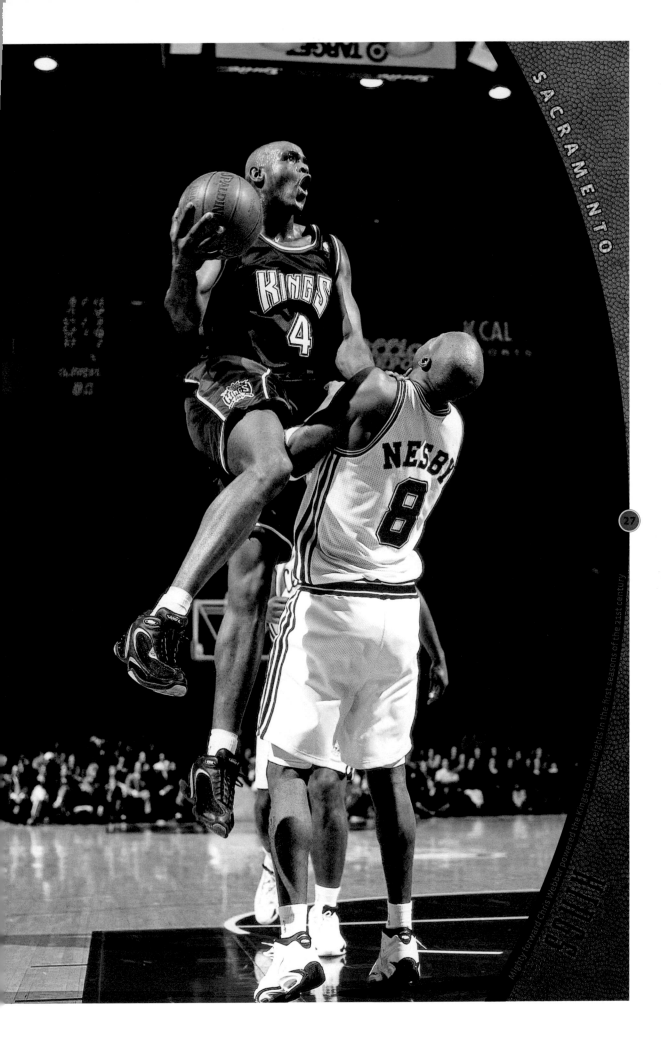

27

Mighty forward Chris Webber powered the Kings to new heights in the first seasons of the 21st century

The Kings acquired Ron Artest, a strapping forward known for his ferocious defense, in a trade in 2006.

Following the 2000–01 season, the Kings swapped Williams for the Vancouver Grizzlies' point guard, Mike Bibby. Bibby—along with Bobby Jackson and Doug Christie—supercharged the Kings' guard lineup with speed and tenacious defense. The team went 61–21 and advanced to meet the two-time defending champion Los Angeles Lakers in the 2002 Western Conference Finals. The series went to a deciding Game 7, but despite the Sacramento crowd's arena-shaking noise, the Lakers prevailed in overtime, 112–106. "We were like boxers, just trying to stay in it for the win," Webber said. "We just didn't get the win."

Three straight winning seasons followed, but the Kings could not get back to the Western Conference Finals, despite the efforts of rising star forward Peja Stojakovic. In 2004–05, general manager Geoff Petrie shook things up by trading away Divac, Christie, and Webber. Still, Sacramento notched a 50–32 record to remain among the NBA's best.

It has been more than five decades since the Kings franchise last ruled as NBA champion. After years of frustration and moving, however, the Kings are clearly heading in the right direction. With the ARCO Arena crowd raising a royal ruckus on a nightly basis, an NBA championship coronation can't be far off.

MASTERMIND OF THE KINGS

As the first-ever draft pick of the Portland Trail Blazers in 1970, Geoff Petrie's flawless shooting and smart decision-making on the court made him one of the NBA's most promising stars. In 1976, though, he was traded away to the lowly Atlanta Hawks with Portland on the cusp of its 1977 NBA championship. Worse for Petrie, a knee injury ended his career before he ever played for Atlanta. But the Princeton University graduate always had a head for the game, and since 1994, he has put that knowledge to work for the Kings. As Sacramento's general manager, Petrie is responsible for all decisions regarding the drafting, trading, and signing of players. "From the moment we met Geoff," said Kings co-owner Joe Maloof, "we knew he was the man to lead our team into the future."

31

Mike Bibby was the heart of the Kings' lineup, frequently sparking the offense with fast-break scores.